W9-CBN-478

THREE
MENNONITE
POETS

THREE
MENNONITE
POETS

Poetry by:

Jean Janzen, U. S. A.
Yorifumi Yaguchi, Japan
David Waltner-Toews, Canada

Good Books®
Intercourse, Pennsylvania 17534

Acknowledgments

"Postcards to My Sister" by Jean Janzen was published in Berkeley Poetry Review, Fall, 1984.
"Sometimes" by Jean Janzen was published in Christianity and Literature (Volume XXXIV, No. 4), Summer, 1985.
"Enough" by Jean Janzen was published in Yankee, September, 1984.
"Once in the Rain" by Jean Janzen was published in Quarry West, Winter, 1986.
"Mennonites in Russia: The Photographs" by Jean Janzen was published in Mennonite Life.
"The Temperature of Cruelty" and "Once in the Rain" by Jean Janzen were published in Direction.
"There Are Days" by Jean Janzen was published in The Christian Leader.
The following poems by Jean Janzen appeared in Words For the Silence, published by the Center for Mennonite Brethren Studies, Fresno, California, 1984: "Mennonites in Russia: The Photographs," "Pastorale," "Saskatchewan Harvest," "Mennonite Music," "Solo," and "These Words Are For You, Grandmother."

The following poems by Yorifumi Yaguchi were published in Poetry Nippon: "Silence," "The Party," "Praying Mantis," "Words," "How to Eat Loaches," "The Beasts," "A Lunchbox," "After My Prolonged Prayer," "Rats," "Devilfish," "A Peasant," and "A Deer."
"Grandpa" by Yorifumi Yaguchi was published in London Magazine, August/September, 1984.
"A Skater" by Yorifumi Yaguchi was published in Christian Living, December 1965.
"A Lonely Season" by Yorifumi Yaguchi was published by Goshen (Indiana) College in Foolscap, 1964.
"Usually," "A Military Song," and "Meditating the Zen Way" were translated from Japanese into English. They first appeared in Senzotachi (Ancestors), a collection of Japanese poems, published by Kyobunsha, Sapporo, 1985.

Several poems by David Waltner-Toews have appeared in the following anthologies and magazines: The Earth is One Body, Good Housekeeping, Mennonite Mirror and Festival Quarterly.

Published by Good Books, Intercourse, PA 17534
Design by Craig Heisey.

Three Mennonite poets.
    Includes index.
    1. English poetry—Mennonite authors. 2. English poetry—20th century. I. Janzen, Jean. II. Yaguchi, Yorifumi, 1932-   . III. Waltner-Toews, David, 1948-   .
PR1178. M45T54 1986 821'.008'092287   86-81460
ISBN 0-934672-38-5
ISBN 0-934672-40-7 (pbk.)

THREE MENNONITE POETS
Copyright © 1986 by Good Books, Intercourse, PA 17534
International Standard Book Number (hardcover): 0-934672-38-5
International Standard Book Number (paperback): 0-934672-40-7
Library of Congress Catalog Card Number: 86-81460

All rights reserved. Printed in the United States of America.
No part of this book may be reproduced in any manner, except for brief quotations in critical articles or reviews, without permission.

Table of Contents

Book One:
Poems by Jean Janzen

About Jean Janzen

Jean Janzen was born December 5, 1933, in Saskatchewan, Canada, to Henry Peter Wiebe and Anna Schultz Wiebe, the seventh child in a family of eight. Her father was a schoolteacher who became a pastor, for which reason they moved to Minnesota in 1939. Her school years were spent in Minnesota and Kansas.

She graduated from Fresno Pacific College with a BA in English and received her Masters in English-Creative Writing from California State University Fresno where she studied with poets Peter Everwine, Philip Levine, and C. G. Hanzlicek.

Her first collection of poems, Words for the Silence (Center for Mennonite Brethren Studies), was published in 1984. Her work is included in a forthcoming anthology, Piece Work, Nineteen Fresno Poets (Silver Skates Publishing, Albany, California). She has also been published by various literary and Christian journals, such as Berkeley Poetry Review, Poet Lore, Quarry West, Radix, Yankee, Festival Quarterly, Christianity and Literature, Christian Century, Mennonite Life, and The Christian Leader.

Jean's husband Louis is a pediatrician in private practice. She has two sons, two daughters, three children-in-law, and a grandson. She also teaches piano and is minister of worship at the College Community Mennonite Brethren Church in Clovis, California.

Separations

All day the separate lakes
of our bodies lap their shores
in secrecy, and when we lie

down to sleep they spill
into the river of our dreams   *mind*
where soul and body meet,

as when we pray, hand
meeting hand, the one   *body - pt. for joining*
that reached up   *together self/soul and*
                               body
against the one that nearly
rooted into the soil
of the lilybed. You can see it
            └ resurrection
in children's eyes the moment
they first awaken, and the way
their hands go out in a slight

motion toward what was there.
Then they rise and stand
beside us. Our hands touch,

but our lakes, all luminous and blue,
are separate, and the vast
fields lie between us.

private experience of body — incarnation of
spirit

Where the Wheat Sways

Around us the summer air
burns and blows so that
where we once stood and kissed

there is no memorial of place.
No one will remember.
Your mother, bent by a tumor

has lain down under this wind.
Old angers live on
like barbed wire holding up

fenceposts, and larks return
to proclaim their territory,
but our moment refuses

to stand up. Who will ever know
that I first saw you in a doorway
surrounded by morning light

here in this spot where the wheat
sways to our hips, where we are
trampling the stalks

which, after we go, will slowly
rise up like witnesses
and fill this space.

The Temperature of Cruelty

We think of the beaten baby
dead against the darkening stain
on the bed, soldiers pulling out
fingernails, the prisoner dangling
for days. But also the years
of bitterness in a family, the cold
turning of the shoulder, the look
that erases you. What is
the temperature of cruelty?
Fire? Boiling oil? Or the great
weight of ice, gravel shearing
rock in a slow grind. Or
that April frost, so lacy
and beautiful, whispering
and biting the orchard to death
in one slow night, when all
the blossoms blacken, and all
that was possible withers
and shatters in the wind.

These Words Are For You, Grandmother

i

I imagine you sitting on the doorstep,
your dark braid undone and rippling
down your back. You are plucking
melodies from the guitar which
he made for you, and he is there
singing along, his arm soft around you
in the Ukrainian dusk. And now it seems
that we are both entering the darkening
house to the pale bed, this bed
of beginnings and endings, of arms
encircling and then letting go,
this bed which you have given me
by your womb.

ii

The crude violin, the little organ
he made of wood scraps and animal bones,
and your guitar are all silent in the room,
the strings untouched. His long hand
slipped from yours after the last embrace,
after his last gathering of the nine
young faces around the terrible bed.
And then the cold light in the room
and the silence, and heaven so far away.
The ministers brought shoes for the children,
flour for your bin. But you were silent,
your eyes empty, your mouth still.

The photograph tells me that I
have eyes and hands like yours
and a mouth with a heavy lower lip.
Look, I am shaping it for words,
making sounds for you. I am speaking
the syllables you couldn't say.
See my breath is pushing away the cold.

iii

After you hanged yourself
they buried you outside the gate
without songs, just a prayer
in the harsh light. My father,
ten years old, had found you
in the barn, your body
a still dark strip, your face
swollen and purple. And by that grave
he could not sing for you;
he did not speak of you.
He sealed his mouth with a heavy stone
and walked away.
And when he held me in his arms
he spoke of rivers
and a black crow against the sky.
Helen of darkness,
I sing you a song.
It is like water from a clear stream,
like a white linen dress.
I take you down, wash you
and comb your hair.
I lay you down beside the man you loved.

iv

The small, abandoned graveyard
lies in tall autumn grass, the markers
tumbled and covered. Last grasshoppers
have gone from the nearby stubbled fields
and a light frost whitens the feathery
heads of foxtail. I have come down
the long narrow road. I have come
with my passport, my photograph
and my name to stand on the unmarked dust
of your body, and there is no sound
but the dry leaves stirring in the alders,
the groaning of roots, and these words
breathing on a page.

[handwritten annotations: "suicide – ultimate rejection of body"; "maternal – muse – face that launches a new quest"; "body not all"; "ancestral stories"; "flesh becomes word"]

Red

The television blooms with fires
in the cities, gunshots, roses

scattered on a kitchen floor.
Two small children and my belly

swollen with another. The summer
sun fills my uterus with radiance;

so much love and violence, the world
gone red. I open my mouth

Like a rose, lay it on the small
foreheads. I wrap my voice

around them, but the syllables
are like a wire fence,

and not one word prevents
the sun or the fire.

*— power in woman's
voice to protect
her generation.
Contrast to her
grandmother's
silence*

I Keep Forgetting

I keep forgetting   *live unaware of body*
that flowers   *or sexual organs are beautiful*
are sexual organs,   *sex is beautiful   flowers*
all those years
my mother reminding   ⌐ *prohibition*
me to keep my legs
together, my dress
down. I bring in
armfuls of them,
arrange bouquets
and place them on
our shining tables.
And when I talk
to you, the velvet
petals lie open
and breathe,   *p. 11 words breathe; poem experiencing body*
and all night
in the patio the jasmine,
so prim and tight,
unspirals itself
to whatever flutters   *orgasm*
against it.

Mennonite Music

Shutting out
the jazz of the world
we made our own music

a strained choral tone
like a taut rope
pulling us through

getting our pitches
from those who knew
breaking into harmonies

and dissonance
and those outside rarely
heard us in our closed places

our tones flattening
into our lives, or did they
now and then perceive

melodies escaping
the ones with wings
flapping softly upward

Solo

Against the swollen sky
the church with its open roof,
great beams over half-broken
walls. An exhalation, a sigh
in the wind.

My grandfather slumps
into the earth; his mouth fills
with dust. His daughter
stands barefoot in the choir.
Her lungs fill with air, vocal
cords tighten in her throat.
Slowly, evenly, the air escapes,   *breathing words becoming flesh*
tones as clear as well water,
vowels so transparent that through them
you can see everything—
what was lost, what remains,   *poems a vision*
what is possible.

Burden

*"The light draws off
As easily as though no one could die
Tomorrow."—Christopher Fry*

Evening sets down a tinted
glass dome on the rim of the world,
and once again you stand
in the doorway calling the children
to supper. One more game, they cry
with voices that splay the air, then
a quick scramble and silence as they
hide in the hedge. You lean heavily
on the doorframe watching the light
change. Late bird calls, stillness,
the ash leaves shiver.

The children huddle closer, their toes
pressing into the fine dust. They cover
their mouths to stifle the sound
of their breathing. They stiffen
with expectation.

And then it is dark. You gather them
into the bright square of the kitchen.
You serve them silently, but you long
to expel a great cry: oh my darlings
with the golden hair, with eyes clear
as water, with your small dark seeds,
deep and divided.

Holding Back

*"Nach das Lachen kommt das Weinen."**
         —German proverb, my mother

This explains
   why I laugh with reserve,
   never plunging in,
   dipping, rather,
   in the shallow end.

You may think
   this one's from the belly,
   that one arcs the night
   like a shooting star.

Believe me,
   I am holding back,
   reserving my breath,
   counting my stitches
   so they'll hold.

No extravagance.
   Money in the bank.
   That is why I open presents
   carefully.
   And when the box is empty,
   I don't cry.

After laughing comes weeping.

Once In The Rain

I explain earth's water cycle
to our son. We lean together
over the page, over the diagram
of life with its curved arrows,

the ocean giving up
a part of itself
in little shivering lines
to the clouds, the child
drinking from a glass;

elemental, unalterable,
except I recall
how once in a warm autumn rain
you took me naked to the deck,

how as I lay curved
in your arms, your dampness
entering all of me,
we dissolved together as if
God had never separated
land and sea,

how we drifted up
over the cedar tips
and the slant of the roof
and hovered there,

how for a long moment
we were certain that
we would never know thirst again.

Burning Apricot Wood

Now we see the tight concentric
rings in the smooth cuts, the orderly
cells that elevated earth's gifts
step by step to the sun,
the patient life-work of wood.
Old Mr. Wells planted the sapling
about the time of Hiroshima
when I was twelve and budding, when
my neighbor was six and last saw
her sister as she left for school
in her uniform carrying her satchel
of papers, the neat rows of Japanese
vocabulary—seed, blossom, apricot.
Last summer the fleshy fruit divided
easily in my palm, juices burst against
the roof of my mouth. And now
the branches burn in my fireplace.
Each wood cell releases its breath
in a flash of apricot heat, all
that had been joined and whole glows
and disintegrates, and the last
exhalations rise into the atmosphere,
into the fiery kisses of the sun.

separation of culture

Mennonites in Russia: The Photographs

i

Picket fences mark the orchard,
the house roof steep and moist.
Martin and Anna Reimer and their seven children
stand by the gate in the half-light
of late afternoon. The pear trees
are glass, curtains at the windows
are frost, and behind them the piano,
not a tremor from its strings.

ii

By the woods thick with alders
the Rosental Choral Society of 1905
holding music folders in white hands,
high collars, cut-out lace,
watch chains across woolen vests,
their mouths in straight lines.
Afterwards they will break into laughter
and touch. They will part
the humming grass with their fine
leather shoes. They will walk
into their homes through doorways
surrounded with thick vines.

iii

Peter David Kroeger stands in his workshop
making his "famous, indestructible clocks."
They have large painted faces
and a pendulum that swings free.
Now they hang all over the world.
One is on my brother's wall in Los Angeles,
The perfect gears mesh cog into cog
every day, his little daughters see
their faces in the brass pendulum,
and when the earth quaked
it made a huge arc,
it went as far as it could.

iv

The pages turn like wheels of a train.
We are going north to Siberia.
My bearded uncle stands up straight
in the crowded cattle car. His suit
is black, his collar white and stiff.
When he speaks, his breath
makes little frozen clouds.
God gave him this land, he says.
He will keep it, he says.
He will lie down in it.

v

Bodies in a long row of wooden boxes
lined with linen, tiny vines
bordering Elizabeth who was raped
again and again. The murderers
are resting in the burned wheat field,
their hands steady as they light
cigarettes. In the hazy distance
the village, the mills broken and silent,
the church with boarded windows
like eyes that have closed.

Curbing The Appetite

They brought them to me
bound in blankets
like cooked sausages,
the fat cheeks bulging
for kisses, their mouths
rooting for my own skin.
I thought of our mother cat
devouring placentas
and umbilical cords,
licking and licking,
barely able to keep
her sharp teeth out
of the soft, flabby necks—
that dark intertwining
of love and possession.

Soon the legs grow long
and sleek, my lips and hands
on their hair and shoulders
grow lighter, loosening.
And then they leave me,
gliding out on black lakes
in their light canoes. I smile,
I wave, I swallow my words.
I eat the spaces between us.

Note To Conrad Grebel From Mt. Pilatus

We take the easy way up, Conrad,
a tram on greased cogs and unbreakable cable.
You would laugh to see us, soft-bellied
and swinging in the blue air. But you too
had your luxuries and an appetite
for the eternal—Greek poetry, Luther's ferment,
and your youthful passions all wrapped into
a brief life. This is your view, the first
to climb and chart this peak. Four hundred sixty
years ago, and yet, against this granite,
only yesterday.

An alphorn sounds against the stone,
its deep tones ricochet from face to face
and fall into the rich valleys. Towns
with towers like the dark tower where your
health broke, where Zwingli, once your friend,
held you for your lofty contradictions,
and you escaped to teach again and to die.

What is the measure of our love?
Is it risk, or endurance? Should I regret
the way I came, a follower, a view unearned?

The air is thin, the edges sharp and clear.
Snowfields deep and glistening around me
are giving themselves away in small streams
and in vapors lifting off. Nothing you
can really measure. Below is the misty valley
with its muddy river where we love, where we
make our choices—you, dropping from the tower
hand over hand, your face luminous in the dark,
and me, holding the rope in my hands. *faith of a follower*

Fittings

for Gail

i

Ever since you arrived
I have been covering you,
as even now I kneel
beside you, pins in my mouth
for the hem. You wail,
it's all wrong; the pins prick
like all the irritations
of my generation.
What you want is to run naked,
or to cover with leaves, you,
my twig, with your strong
slender foot, your small hard buds,
your shining eyes.

ii

November sun lowering, silk
of your wedding dress over
your shoulder blades, the basted
rows of tucks on your breasts.
In the dusky room the cut pieces
are feathers on your skin.
The soup is simmering, hunters
on their way home, and you
are shivering in pieces of silk,
the full gathered sleeves
opening like wings.

iii

By now you know that nothing
really covers you, or does it
truly fit. Love outgrows
its newest clothes, and what
we finally wear is a patchwork
of the given and the taken.
In the hospital morgue the bodies
I saw wore nothing but a tag
on one big toe, their shirts
limp in the closet. I want you
to fold my dresses then
and give them away, and to think
of me young again, running naked
through wet and shining fields.

Saskatchewan Harvest

i

All that is left of my birthplace
is the front doorstep
and a few rocks from the cistern.
Place of first cry, first light
now filled with the lace of yarrow and clover,
the various grasses running in the wind,
and in the space of my parents' bed
a small, wild willow
rooting like a placenta. — *growth from place*

ii

I find the old hedge of lilacs
where we played house,
my sister and I marking rooms
with string:

      Here is the stove
      with the dandelion pie
      here is the crib
      and the lullaby

      here is the needle
      here is the thread
      here are the leaves
      drifting into my head

      here is the snowfall
      here are my bones
      here are my father's arms
      lifting me home.

iii

Filling in like a tapestry,
these people, this place,
this northern prairie
white with the long light
of summer, the snow upon snow
of winter. But the figures — *hint at suffering, work*
are dark, the faces intent—
farmers driving their sweating horses,
children pulling sleds

piled high with wood, women
bending over babies
and kneading troughs
beside the bloody hook,
the open carcass of the pig—
like a Brueghel, except these figures
do not play or drink; they sit
in straight rows inside churches
that are long and plain.
Under its armor of ice
the Saskatchewan River scrapes
on silt, poplars
shiver together on the slopes,
and there is the shining, almost a glare,
and some faces with open mouths, singing.

iv

The granaries holding wheat
are filled with music and light,
for all through the long summer days
these small kernels drank it in,
swelling with the calls of meadowlarks,
the syncopation of rain,
the silver dance of Northern Lights.

To be a child again,
to tie cardboard wings
to my arms and fly
from the rafters
and then glide into the sea
of slippery grain, my whole body
immersed in harvest—
the best of it—   *memories of the core/best*
the chaff all blown away.

Enough

Another evening
folding its wings
among the ash trees,
a wind stirring
the darkening spaces.

My mother asks
did I love you
enough?
She quilts with a very
sharp needle
making tiny close
stitches around
the flying geese,
fastening them down
to muslin.

Her hands are becoming
translucent.
Sometimes I see them
float away,
her whole body
becoming loose and free,

but now
the knots, the clipped
threads, the shadows
in the reeds.

Sometimes

Sometimes
when the sun
is overhead
and we lie
in its great outpouring,
our skins evaporate
and our bones become
light and airy.

We are alone in this.
The garden continues
to drink the earth,
stalks leaning heavily
with blooms,
sycamores extending
and thickening into
silent shade.

Only we can see
that the sky
is coming nearer,
that it is wearing
a new iridescence
at its rim,
and we know
with a certainty
that we are not made
for earth,
a feeling
that already
with hair burning
we rise.

p. 18 Once in the rain

Ionian Sea

Here in the sand
we can feel it,
how our feet dissolve
in the warm, lapping waves,
how even marble
disintegrates.

Looking into your eyes,
blue and lambent,
I fail to imagine
the death stare, yet
I know that with one gasp
you could slip away
as easily as a fish,
and I would stand here
alone wearing this tight
wedding band given
in ignorance
like so much that is given,
the sculptor surprised
at what his chiseling
gives back, and no way
to undo it.

One block of time,
this moment, the sandpipers
racing in and out.

Pastorale

Dawn over farmland,
over the endless blanket
of new wheat. Gray-green
distances. The rounded hills
like hips and shoulders
of giants asleep.
The highway curves past
farm kitchens where families
lean over plates of eggs, listening
to news of prices and assassinations.

Morning grows bolder now.
Flick of oriole, the grackle's
green wing. The fields
shine and sway. Jeremiah,
arthritic and groaning, turning
in his damp bed to take
the warmth of the sun.

To My Aunt Dying In Autumn

You are a fallen leaf turning
to paper, the leaf one finds
after winter, a lacework of veins.
I lift you carefully to turn you
on the sheepskin, but even then
the parchment over your hipbone
cracks and opens. Your lips
move without a sound.

Here in the north, snow is already
falling with sudden wind gusts
lifting it back to the steely sky.
At the darkening window I see
the reflected bulk of my middle-aged
body, branches whipping into
its thickness. I remember
how I waited for breasts and hips
to round the thin rope of girl
I was, for that first drop of blood
on the tissue, a tiny bell trembling
inside of me. This summer
I heard it again in an English meadow
at Hadrian's wall where we walked.
A flock of sheep, lambs with a ting,
ting, by a wall that keeps nothing out
or in, under a sky that whitens everything
except the sound of something
small and silver, ringing.

Hair

Reassuring against
the tips of our fingers,
brushing against
our loneliness.

One whole semester
in eighth grade history class
I resisted running my hand
over Pete's butch
in front of me, thick
and flat as a brush.
So many heads I haven't
touched.

Hair whispers, says
we never love enough.
We cut it short, and still
the soft lips lean out
and sigh. Under our clothes
it murmurs, outlives
our skin.

Dad, your sheen of silver.
Mother, the dark silks
of it against your cheekbone.
My love, my sons, daughters,
friends, I stroke your hair,
all the hollow shafts
waiting to be filled.

Postcards To My Sister

i

Touring the cathedral today
I thought of how often
I lay beside you trying in vain
to fall asleep, chanting
scriptures in alphabetical order:
All we like sheep have gone astray,
how I stayed awake through Z,
my nerves zinging with *Seek ye the Lord*
while he may be found—the terror
of losing him, that he might hide
from a searching child, and if I found him,
that I would die in the glory.
Child of the Dark Ages,
chipping away at my block of stone.

ii

In Sorrento beside an ancient vineyard
in a modern hotel, I should be calm,
the cool tile under my feet, curtains
soft and swinging like a baby's dress,
and a stillness like the stillness
of you and me together, barefoot
on the linoleum on a muggy summer day
just before the storm, the one which tore
the lilacs, the one with the thunder
which broke loose and avalanched
into our simple orderly room.

iii

If you had been with me in the art gallery
you would have felt it, too, what we missed,
barren as we were of Turners and Rembrandts,
only calendars from the First National Bank
and a motto, Keep Looking Up. And yet,
as I gazed, I recognized our rare possession,
the harmony of our singing, all ten of us
around the piano, the balance of it, radiant
skies of "Crown Him with Many Crowns,"
"He Leadeth Me" with its pastoral greens

and its fetid valleys of death, the rising
clouds, the shafts of light.

iv

Sunning by the pool
I watched them today,
the young and easy ones
moving steadily through
the water in silken rhythms
which you and I, untaught,
will only accomplish in heaven
one day. The breathless thrashing
finished once and for all,   *body in heaven*
we'll move with utter grace
and we will emerge confident,
our hair slicked back
from our perfect faces,
our firm thighs glistening
before the eyes of the Lord.

v

The lake by the cemetery
shimmers like crinkled foil,
peonies are watercolor pink
along the graveled walk
by the maple trees with their
pale and delicate leaves.
There is a lightness
in our hometown, feathers
in the air, an obligato of happiness.
Then why am I hearing a moaning
(you would hear it, too)
a slow groaning of roots, or maybe
from the depth of the lake
the bones of the dead are humming   *ancestral voice*
in unison, holding the pitch
for the beginning of an anthem.

vi

Today as I sat alone in the park,
evening gathered in the elms,
and couples walked by arm in arm
away from me, away in their private joy,
and suddenly I was back in our bedroom
watching you at the mirror as you combed
your rich brown hair and dabbed
Evening in Paris on your earlobes and wrists,
and then I was leaning over the bannister
to see him touch you, to hear the easy laughter,
the screen door slamming shut, your heels
tapping evenly away from me.

vii

I have decided that the dead are more visible
than the living—these looming memorials,
eternal flames steady even in the rain.
Maybe it is this lion in Lucerne
who has convinced me. Carved out
of a granite wall, he will weep
for generations. Little boys stroke
his paws lightly, and at night they dream
that they have disturbed him. They feel
his breath in their necks, and cry out
at his awful roar.

Tomorrow I will light candles
in the cathedral in a drafty corner
by the old stones, one for you, one for me.
Brief flames, sputtering, leaning.
Nothing to show but a pool of melted wax.

There Are Days

There are days   *contrast w/ other days of not knowing*
when I believe in
the reconciliation of old walls,   — *break down barriers,*
in stone fences giving up   —   *echo "Separation"*
to the weather,
when calla lilies   *resurrection*

are white flags
and all the grass bends
to the southern wind,

days when doors open,
the table set for tea,
telegrams arriving

that say I am loved
just as I am,   — *hymn of confession, conversion*
when I loosen my grip

on the cup, set it down,
turn up my palms,   — *opening to spirit — like hands in*
and they bloom like crocuses.   *"Separation"*

THREE
MENNONITE
POETS

Book Two:
Poems by Yorifumi Yaguchi

To Beth

About Yorifumi Yaguchi

Yorifumi Yaguchi was born November 1, 1932 in
Ishinomaki, Miyagi Prefecture, Japan. He graduated
from Tohoku Gakuin University with a B.A. in
English, from International Christian University
with an M.A. in Education, and from Goshen Bibli-
cal Seminary with a B.D. in theology.

He spent one year as American Council of
Learned Societies Visiting Scholar at the State Uni-
versity of New York, Buffalo, and recently taught a
semester at Shenyang, China. Yaguchi is presently
professor of American poetry in the literature de-
partment of Hokusei Gakuen College.

With his Christian faith as its foundation, Yagu-
chi writes poetry in both English and Japanese. He
has published two collections of English poems, A
Shadow and How to Eat Loaches, plus five volumes
of Japanese poetry, some of which has been trans-
lated. His work has also appeared in poetry maga-
zines in England, Australia, India, and the U.S.A.

Yaguchi and his wife Mitsuko live in Sapporo,
Hokkaido with sons Yobu and Yujin. Yaguchi is lay
pastor of the Shalom Mennonite Church.

Yorifumi Yaguchi

A Skater

Somebody crossed
The icy-field in me
By the sharpest edge,
Just now!

Surprised,
I turned my head
Into it quickly
But it's too late,

And only two lines
Were left continuous
Beyond the horizon on
The ice on which nobody
Had ever passed.

Praying Mantis

This morning I saw a male
praying mantis being
eaten by his female.

I could almost hear his
wild shout of ecstasy
as his wife ate him

and his joy seemed to increase
the more as his body was
violently bitten along.

The complete trance of
self-oblivion came at the moment
when his last part was bitten.

—Tonight when I am exhausted
after our long and
violent intercourse,

I think of the male mantis,
wondering if his swallowed body
was digested or is still praying in her.

After My Prolonged Prayer

After my prolonged prayer I lift up my eyes . . .
And find, to my confusion, a fat,
Pig-like beast standing just in front at me;
It peels its eyes red toward me in a familiar manner.

—Ah, unmistakably, it is the incarnation
Of what had secretly been hiding deep within me,
Which quickly jumped out of my mouth
In the form of prayer a moment ago.

Because of its ugliness, I try hard to turn
My eyes away from that, which approaches me most
Affectionately, trying hard to touch me
with its long red organ dangling like a bell.

The Party

"Seems some child is crying
In a far, far place," they say with
Smiles over the champagne, and their party
Grows gay with the music of their band
Raising its volume up to
Try to kill that cry.

Then, well-shaped gentlemen begin to
Dance with ladies with half-naked,
Mounted breasts. Chandeliers shine
Like many suns with the marble floor
Flashing like a mirror

"Oh, how beautiful! Oh,
How . . ."

>They do not hear any more,
>they who dance, laugh and are intoxicated
>Hear no more the cry of a child in a far,
>Far land. They hear no more
>The explosions of
>Guns, grenades and bombs they made.

They are dancing, elegantly
Smiling, gradually embracing each other
More tightly and continue to
Dance through the night.

Grandpa

Grandpa suddenly gets up at midnight and
shouts, "It's time!" and
throws off our *futon** and makes us get up and
sit in line in the living room.

After calling our names, he sits
before his desk with the blackboard behind and
begins giving a lecture he had repeated
for thirty years at a university.

We have to take notes on whatever he tells us,
because during his lecture
he checks our notes carefully and
scolds us if they are not satisfactory.

His clouded eyes glitter,
his bent back straightens and
his moustache trembles like a float.
But the lecture finishes too soon.

He collapses and starts snoring, pissing
in his pants, his snot forming a bubble
on the end of his nose, and repeating in his sleep,
'The Kamikaze are coming!'

*Japanese bedding

Usually

I love peace
but when I wear a soldier's uniform,
I begin to wish a war would happen
and to feel like killing
as many enemies as possible
by raiding them, if so ordered,
and dying willingly
for the sake of the Emperor
and our country.

How to Eat Loaches
—Some people say raw loaches are good
for the heart . . .

You just swallow
the loaches living
without chewing them.

They fall right
into your stomach where
they moan, struggle and

try to jump out.
But they gradually become
faint and still

like mice in a
snake or a minority race
in a society.

Silence

in a far
place
i do not even know
a
leaf
falling down
like a silence
on the mirror
of a lake
making few
wavelets
hardly seen

ah
that sound
disturbs
my silence
like the explosion
of a
temple bell

The Beasts

Finally tearing off the chain, a beast rushed
Violently out of a boy
Up behind a girl fixing tea,
Thrusting her down,
Stripping her,
And began
To lick her body.

>Astonished, the boy tried hard
>To seize the beast from behind,
>But was easily thrown away,
>While the girl soon lost her strength to
>Struggle, falling down.

But at this moment! another beast leaped
Out of this girl, and the beasts began
To fight each other, up and down,
Biting with fangs,
Growling, scratching,
Slobbering over
The hair of their bodies,

>While the boy and the girl barely
>Escaped into the corner of the room, where
>They are watching, trembling in fear,
>Their endless, fierce fight
>For the first time in their lives.

In the Wood. . . .

a.

I have happened to come to myself
Among wave-like sounds of leaves,
And I have found out that
Trees were continuously whispering to me
And that I was nodding to them continuously.

b.

These branches
And those branches
Are sounding continuously like waves. . . .
No, these are not the sounds of leaves
But the secret throbbings of hearts of
Children who are hiding among trees.

c.

Wind is passing.
Between branches,
Shaking their leaves softly, and
When I am looking at it,
I cannot but believe that
Wind and leaves are
Whispering together
Secretly and
Affectionately.

d.

Why do you so much attract children,
O trees?
Look,
So many children
Approach you and
Are looking at you
Silently,
Forgetting time.

e.
Trees were good friends to birds,
But children were lonesome
For trees were sullen to them.

But one day children ventured to
Speak to them, which answered them back
With unceasing loquacity.

f.
One day a child lost its way in a wood,
So it was sitting on the root of a tree,
Looking up above the sky, in which
A Siberian kite was easily flying.

While looking at it for a long,
Long time, it has become itself a
Tree without its even a slightest notice.

g.
Children are climbing up,
Climbing up and up the tree.
They never stop in the middle,
But climb up toward the higher top.

They are never scared to stop
On a thin top, but
Are climbing above it,
Climbing up and up straight onto the sky.

h.
Children are secretly
Looking at me
Among branches,
Behind leaves,
With their crystal eyes
Shining.
There, just above
My shoulders, just
Beside my foot, they
Are looking at me,
Hiding themselves, and
I can hear their breath
More clearly than a wind.

i.
Children, children, you
Run like an echo
Into the interior of the wood,
With a shout of joy which I cannot hear,
Leaping into the world, into which
I cannot go, and your voices are
Coming toward me as if
From a world a thousand years ago.

A Fish

In the rock
a big fish,
still as a stone,
strains its ears,
trying hard to
learn how it's
going outside,

while outside,
I
stand immobile,
holding my breath,
trying hard to
learn how it's
going inside.

A Lonely Season

The day is dying down,
And the children are going home,
Then the world quiets down as in the wood.

That is all. . . .
But why does my heart ache so much?

Look at the face of this child,
Left alone by the roadside,
Standing vacantly in the darkness
Which is rapidly growing up to surround him
Like a wall.
Look at its face,
It has no crossness any more
Which it had while playing with the children.
But the loneliness is
Flowing out of the face.

The night is falling upon him,
But the child is not going home.
Everybody is going home
Hurriedly
Even with tears on their cheeks,
But this child is not going home.

The child is gazing,
Leaning against the pillar,
Doing nothing,
But only gazing
In the mirror
At the face of its mother,
Which is gradually changing into
A face of some other woman.

After its mother is gone out,
The child is looking
Through the window at
The darkness, in which
Nothing is seen.
It is looking,
Never moving from the windowside,
Nor talking back,
Nor smiling back,
But only gazing
At the darkness of
The outside world.

A Lunchbox

Just as there is a toilet in every house,
There is a lunchbox of dung in every man:
Golden, soft dung, blue, inkish dung,

Brown dung mixed with fish bones,
Black, hard dung like stones,
Red dung stuck hard to the box, etc., etc.

See these lunchboxes neatly arranged
In the loins of those ladies
Sitting good mannered in the seats on the bus.

The boxes shake as the bus shakes,
And the feces shake up and down, right to left,
And sing with and without sound.

If any has too much of it,
It leaks out in puffs, though she tries
Hard to close her lips tight.

A

withered leaf
hanging on a twig
heavy as the earth

Words

Leave them there
in the darkness

as they have been
from the beginning.

It's their silences
that speak to us

and not
the combined sounds.

A Military Song

When I am alone in a quiet place,
I find myself humming
to myself a military song
learned when I was a child.

I think I am the
absolute pacifist
but in spite of my intention,
the song springs up

naturally out of my depth . . .
whenever I am unguarded or absent-minded.

Many Winds

Many winds
swarm to
a wounded word,
picking at it
like vultures

until it becomes
a white bone,
half buried in the
sand, and sharpens
into a razor.

A Rescued Vietnamese Boy

For days we did not eat or drink.
Babies sucked withered breasts,
feebly crying, while my brother suddenly
burst into laughter and jumped into the sea . . .

Then one dawn we found a big fishing boat,
a Japanese one, near us, and we waved
and shouted, *"Tasukete!",** the word
Japanese salesmen taught us before the liberation . . .

But the boat, pretending not to notice us,
quickly went away and we were again floating
without any country to return to or to go to
and my family died one after another . . .

*_"Save us!"_

Rats

One day a few blood-stained rats
Jumped suddenly out of my mouth and
Quickly ran away, as I gasped to watch them.

I looked into my stomach in a hurry,
And there! my intestines were all
Gone! but innumerable rats were running

Around, eating up everything.
"I've got to get rid of them before it's too late!"
I said to myself, almost fainting with horror.

But then, they began to jump up out of my mouth,
One after another, and when I shut my jaws,
I bit into a swollen one, which dangles from my teeth.

Gravestones

I caught some words,
which were raging hard
in my hands to flee away,

     but finally I pinned them
     down on a sheet of paper.

There they were writhing,
groaning in their death agony,
under the pins of letters,

     but gradually their wings stopped convulsing
     and they were changed into gravestones.

A Woman

naked
is lying
deep
in the grass
on a mountain
with the red
full
moon
between her
thighs

That Child. . . .

     That child is never attached to me,
     How long the time may pass and
     Whatever I may do, never
     Will it be attached to me, and
     I know in it the flame of malice
     Is burning up like a freezing ice.

With friendship I try to approach it,
Then it boils hostility like an oil and
Draws back step by step, and should I
Approach more, it begins to peel its
Big, red eyes in its soiled face, and
Attacks me in full hatred with a stick
In one hand and mud in the other.

     That child is never attached to me,
     How long the time may pass and
     Whatever I may do, never
     Will it be attached to me, and
     I know in it the steel of
     Bad temper is blowing like a whirlwind.

So finally I give it up and leave it alone,
Then the more its crossness grows and it
Lets passing children cry, hits them with
Blue veins in its forehead, and to approaching
Adults it throws pebbles with nonsense cry, and
At length, with tears full of its face, it
Dashes toward me with stones in its hands.

> That child is never attached to me,
> How long the time may pass and
> Whatever I may do, never
> Will it be attached to me, and
> I know in it loneliness
> Lies in the form of desert.

At night I try to take a peep
Into its room through the closed door,
And it is crying, clenching its teeth
Hard, trying not to utter crying voice,
And its leaf-like hands are
Hardened into iron and are tearing off
Without its notice the sheet on its bed.

But should I try to go in the room
To console it, it all at once
Stops to cry and raids me most
Furiously with its nails and brutal cry.

> That child is never attached to me,
> How long the time may pass, and
> Whatever I may do, never
> Will it be attached to me, and
> I know in it solitude
> Is glittering like hungered eyes.

In the Wood

Leaves piling up at their feet,
the trees stand naked. There is no
wind shaking the branches, no birds chirping.

Standing here, I hear a streamlet
creeping quietly like a snake,
a sound I never noticed during green times.

Meditating the Zen Way
(translated by Mary C. Miller)

Deep in the mountains
high on a rock I meditate zen fashion
concentrating on the gentle movement of
leaves in the trees and gradually
sinking into oblivion, when

Brr, brr, brr, brrrr, brrr, a formation of
helicopters flies over, shaking the trees
Controlling myself—the copters will pass on
like a rain shower—I again take up my zen
posture—but, brr, brr, brr, brrrr, brrr, again—

"Clear your mind of mundane thoughts and
fire will be cool to the touch"—unlike the
monk's famous koan, nor able to attain to
the zen wisdom "Sound is also silence,"
I jump to my feet and

Shake my fist at the copters
"Get outa here, dammit!
How can ya do zen with all that!"
Maybe they can't hear me, but
they can read my gestures—

Without the slightest notice of me
brr, brr, brrr, brrrr
they come on, until passing overhead
some soldiers look down and
wave back

A Deer

The bullets explode
and the powder smoke envelops
the trees in a far wood
in my sleep

And I am half dreaming of my sweetheart
and half hearing those faint sounds of
shooting and the confused footsteps of those
fleeing in all directions

And when all those sounds fade away
into the mud of my drowsiness,
suddenly!
breaking the curtain of resumed calmness

One wounded deer desperate
comes rushing toward me
with its eyes bloodshot
out of breath finally

Jumping violently into me
shattering
my peace and ease of drowsiness
irredeemably

I Remember. . . .

I remember that
The first street-girl I saw
Was the sister of my good friend.
She had come to our house several times
During the war, when we suffered from the shortage
Of food, bringing us some vegetables and rice
And she was fourteen or fifteen when I saw her on the street,
And she was a short, baby-faced girl.

I remember that
My friend was weeping
When we saw his sister
Walking along with an armed soldier
Hand in hand in the street.
His eyes were swollen with tears,
His hands were trembling
And his face was changed into white as a paper.

I do not know where she is
And what she is doing now,
Living or dead, happy or unhappy,
But my friend
Killed himself,
Throwing himself down a steep cliff,
Soon after we saw that scene.

A

drop
from the moon . . .

and the end-
less

spreading a-
cross the pond . . .

faintly shaking the
waterlilies

one
after another

Devilfish

One day my little son began to writhe in agony,
crying out, "My stomach hurts." So, against
the sunshine I held up his naked body to
look through and there! devilfish
tearing his soft, rosy flesh with its legs of
barbed wires. His blood runs into them incessantly.

At the sudden sunshine, devilfish holds its
breath, watching hard outside, with its eyes
spitting darkness and staring straight into my eyes.

Even as I stand watching, I can no longer tell
which is his flesh and which devilfish, but
from his flesh its legs come out one after another,
rapidly growing big and strong.

I Saw a Soldier

I saw a soldier as old as my father
Stealthily picking up like a chicken
One grain of rice after another, which
Were fallen and scattered in a stream,
And his uniform was as withered as
A dried cabbage.

And I saw an officer as young as my brother
With a long sword chiming,
With long, shiny, black boots squeaking,
With a new military dress on with medals glittering,
With a fat, apple-like face shining,
With big, mountain-like shoulders perking up,
With a chicken-breast,
Like a proud tiger
Among small scared cats.

A Peasant

Ask anyone behind my back:
"Look at his feet straddle flat ground,"
They'll say; "Listen to his sing-song
Whine," they'll say.

So my father and his,
and his before: all peasants,
all a few moments of mirth
for the city-bred kind.

So I left my home town,
got an education,
tried to level my tongue
to Tokyo speech,

became a teacher in a city,
But veneer wears off,
the coarse wood shows through,
and though I wear a tie

my own sap now shoots at me,
"Hey, Yorifumi, you are rotting!
What are you trying to fit yourself to?
Come back to the soil,

Be a peasant again. If not,
nothing but water will run through you!"

THREE
MENNONITE
POETS

Book Three:
Poems by David Waltner-Toews

About David Waltner-Toews

David Waltner-Toews was born May 29, 1948, in Manitoba, Canada, to Russian-born Mennonite parents. He was educated first as a writer, then as a veterinarian, and most recently as an epidemiologist. Currently David is working as a veterinary epidemiologist in Indonesia, while continuing to write essays, poetry, and fiction.

He has been published in Canadian magazines and journals (he was a regular contributor to Harrowsmith magazine), and anthologized in Canada, the United States, Great Britain, and East Germany. Three collections of his poetry have appeared: That Inescapable Animal (Pinchpenny Press, Goshen (IN) College, 1974), The Earth is One Body (Turnstone Press, Winnipeg, 1979), and Good Housekeeping (Turnstone Press, Winnipeg, 1983).

David and his wife, Kathy, have two children. David is a member of the Rockway Mennonite Church, Kitchener, Ontario.

Legs

My legs occasionally tire
of being legs   toting
my torso around
like a couple of coolies
They want to topple
like trees   deep
in the forest   with a slow moan
They want to wiggle
their roots   kicking
up a cloud of leafy sheets
They want to build a log cabin
log over log
rooted at the corner

My legs want to live
with your legs
They want to discuss Plato
and his theory of caves
They are tired of being separated
having the wool pulled over them
kept in the prickly dark
They want to discuss roots
They want to discover
where your legs come from
they want to go somewhere
with your legs
to run a race   sideways

Later   they will stand
next to your legs in the shower
and they will feel good again
about just being legs

Sweeping

the snow was expected
we were not prepared
for the blizzard

the trees like stiff brooms
quivered
against gray clouds
compulsively tidying
the sky

like trees we stood
out in the swirling
snow

sweeping

sweeping

Christmas, 1979

No one
is at the door

My father steps in
when I reach out
to check the mail
He bends down
to remove his galoshes

I had not thought
to invite him this Christmas
He has been dead
almost a year

He takes off
his overcoat   After dinner
he sits in the big green
easy chair   reading stories
to my son
Old MacDonald had a farm
The boy laughs
My father laughs

I come from the kitchen
a piece of cold turkey
in my hand
My father looks comfortable
as if he intends to stay
a long time

An Explosion of Ice

an explosion of ice
so close
the cold shards slice
between my ribs

where he was   a black hole
Sucked toward it   I
am stretched   distorted   pulled
apart
The space is never filled
constellation shattered

The minister lips cheerfully
of victors and overcoming
This can only be a triumph
from some vantage point
across the unimaginable black
chasm
for me no victory at all

I cannot imagine
this body not doing
am undone
by the sallow   stopped head
I cannot disarticulate myself
from this event

Here is my father
black curly hair   stocky frame
the flaming optimist
Here is the still-warm body
on the X-ray table   Oh Papa Papa
here is my ribcage
drifting in space
one
small ember
glowing
in its gleaming
claw

Emmanuel

thousands of fathers dead before are no comfort
in the presence of my dead father

promises of golden mansions   deformed angels
bubble gum and trumpets are no consolation

these religious politicians who speak of sleep
to their adoring lambs   they do not know
my God   my dark forsaken God

the only comfort after volcanic ruptures
skies split by lightning and the thunderous
toppling of heaven's gilded pillars is this

dead silence of wood and wet rock
and the solitary punctuation of a frog
like a comma   promising

The Door

for John and Eleanor

My father worked with horses
as a boy
tugging the great sweating rumps
along a straight furrow

Later he worked in the church
though I would be unkind
to draw the obvious parallel

He turned just as he left
the sun in his eyes
so that he had to shade them
with his hand
He waved and smiled
I could see the black-maned horses
glistening with sweat
streaked with dust
The field was not quite done

He was gone

The body suddenly ungiving
The sun extinguished
a field cast
into chill darkness

It is not sleep
no slick and golden road
to glory   The body's carriage
shockless and numb
left shattered by the way
death is death is death
the slow walk to what is
I AM

All words are vanity
revolutions benedictions bombs three cheers for
these repetitions
all in vain
In the end the door opens
Someone is there   a guide perhaps

Baby Love

*for Rebecca, no longer a baby, nor so easily
deceived*

The vacuum cleaner has a blunt   brown body
He lives on dirt   His jokes are shoddy

Baby follows the longnosed beast
trailing crumbs   She's looking pleased

The beast loves fuzz and old brown socks
The baby loves the way he walks

The baby wants to hold his nose
She thrills at how it sucks and blows

She thinks   watching him tucked away
she'll have to marry him   someday

Tante Tina's Lament

Hänschen is a fool
and I am his mother,
Lord forgive us both.
Hänschen struts about the city
like a chicken.
He wears a pink shirt
and plaid, big-bottomed *hosen*.
When he was little,
his bottom was like a *zwieback*.
I spanked his little buns
and how he crowed!

Now he wags his tongue at me
and thinks I am ignorant.
He says farmers have no brains
they should all be businessmen.
He says farm girls don't know how to walk
and I don't know how to barbecue a steak.
Oh his heart is full of *borscht*
and his words are sour.
Don't call me Hänschen, he says.
My name is John.
Do I not know my son's name?
Did I not argue for six nights
with David, my husband, about that name?

On Wednesday night
the young people go to church.
They eat *platz* and give testimonies.
The girls have long golden hair.
Their cheeks are rosy from harvest
and dresses cover their knees.
When the young people sing together
it is heaven above and earth below
with sopranos and basses.

But my Hänschen
goes to dance in the city.
He has a girl friend.
She smears grease on her lips.

Her blond hair is cut and curled
and her knees are bare
like a young calf.
When they dance
their legs are noodles
and the music is a tractor.
The girl friend says it is not a shame
for a woman to cut her hair.
She thinks Mennonites are like Hutterites
and has never heard of *roll kuchen*.
What good can come of that?

Hänschen says she is a modern girl.
He says we must speak English to her
because she goes to the United Church.
He says Low German is a pile of manure.
Listen here, my little boy.
I will surround you with Low German.
I will speak piles of it to you.
Then you will know what Low German is!
Then you will remember
a mother's anger is a willow switch.

He does not listen.
We are poor, he says.
We do not know how to make money.
He wants to be rich, like the English,
and save us all from *Mannagruetze*.
His heart is tight as a peppernut.
His head is a *piroshki*
stuffed with fruit.

In the barn, the cats eat mice
and wait for milking time.
When my man comes in
I serve him dinner, steaming on a plate.
But my son does not know happiness.

On New Year's Eve
we go to church at night,

and on Easter
as the sun rises
we sing praises.
Hänschen is at church by eleven
on Easter.
On New Year's Eve
he goes to dance.
He does not come to hear the children
on Christmas Eve!
When he was still a *bursch*
he was a wise man in the play.

Oh my son
my heart is heavy,
thick as *glums*.
If you come home
it will rise, light and sweet.
I will make you *porzelky* for breakfast
and we will celebrate the New Year
every morning.

Friday Night

Friday night sits in the closet
all week long   head in hands
waiting for the week to be over
He hopes no one has to be at work
this Saturday   He hopes
the day was okay and is glad
when the children go to bed early
He hopes everybody isn't
too tired
He hopes they will be able to find him
here   hiding behind the bathrobes
He hears the closet door open
Clearing his throat
he straightens his collar
Someone is reaching
for the hanger in front of him
He grins   foolishly

Hänschen's Success
(Poor Immigrant Makes Good)

"But alas for you who are rich!"
cried the old blue denims.
Having outgrown them
I stuck them into a paper bag
and took them to the Mennonite Relief Store.
The gray-haired clerk
crinkled them open like an old songbook.
"What have we here?" he sang.
I shrugged my shoulders.

An iron-on seat patch glared at me.
"You have had your time of happiness!"
it shouted.
　"What was that?"
asked the old man, cupping his ear.
I headed for the door.
"Yes I'm sure they'll bring someone
happiness," he said, checking the pockets.

Out on the street
my corduroys hugged me.
I thrust my palms into their pockets
and we held hams
all the way home.
That night, religiously,
I hung them like a prayer
in my closet.

The next day my bells and I
were out strolling and they whispered
snugging up against my thigh,
"You know, a man that has
really ought to have more
don't you think?"
Well, it's not every day a man's pants
give him that kind of freedom!

We swung into a store
and before you could say Sunday morning
there was a whole choir of cords
humming in my closet.
Now, when I swing open the door
in the morning
it's like a Hallelujah chorus in cotton
singing me out into the day.

"Praise the Lord!" shouts the chorus.
"Thank you that we are not blue.
Thank you for this free country
where a man can rise above his jeans."
Thus, every day, scripture and my thighs
are fulfilled and I respond: "Dear Lord,
My heart pants for thee.
Hallelujah. Amen."

Hänschen's Blues

I am a father
and Johnny is my fool
God help him.
He swaggers like an Indian
in striped coveralls
and heavy leather boots.
He shuffles like his feet are cast in bronze.
When he was just a tyke
he wore the finest shoes.
I've had *them* bronzed
and set above the fireplace.

His tongue is a hundred dollar check
written on a one dollar brain account.
He says businessmen have no heart,
they should all be farmers.
He says city girls are prissy
and don't know how to make yogurt.
His head is like a steak,
tough and overdone.
Don't call me, he says, I'll call you.
How cutely he used to call me Papa!
Now he thinks
his father is a lending agency—
interest free!

On Wednesday night
the young people meet at our house.
They drink Seven-up and swim in the pool.
The girls keep their curls above the water.
They bat their eyelashes
and show off new ensembles.
Later, the boys bring out guitars
and they all sing Jesus songs,
bouncy and clean as newborn babies.

But my appleseed
goes to barn dances.
He has a girl friend
who says hair spray is unnatural.
Her hair is long and straggly.

She wears bluejeans
with patches on the seat.
When they dance
they stomp their feet and whoop
like a bunch of farmers.
The girl friend thinks Mennonites
wear big black hats.
She says Hutterites are with it
and has never seen a Hymn Sing on T.V.
What kind of bringing up did she have?

Johnny says she is a modern girl.
He says we should be kind to her
because she's from Toronto.
He says education is for fools.
He should know: I sent him
all the way through college,
the little wise guy.
I should have taken him behind a barn
and thrashed him with a textbook.
Then he would know what education is!

His ears are full of wax.
We are too rich, he says.
We don't know how to live right.
He wants to be poor, like the Indians,
and save us all from income tax.
His heart is fake as a wooden nickel.
His head is an empty pocket
with holes torn in it.

On the patio
my English sheepdog chews a milkbone
and my wife reads
Future Shock.
But my son is discontented.

On New Year's Eve
we have church people over
and on Easter
we donate chocolates

to the Sunday School.
Johnny has a peace vigil
Easter morning.
On New Year's Eve
he goes to dance.
He doesn't even come to hear the kids
on Christmas Eve!
When he was still wet behind the ears
he was a shepherd in the play.

Oh my boy,
what do you know about the price of land?
the dirt-floored houses and potato soup
we struggled out of?
If you come home
I'll plant a garden in the back lawn.
You can pull thistles every weekend.
And I'll never once, God help me, mention money.

Grocery List
for Wilma and Barry

In buying groceries   as in life
one must have a list
and the list must be transcended

One day   for instance   red peppers
bright as a choir of children
may be singing among the vegetables
They may remind me of my son
and I will buy them all
just to make me happy   and to make
sweet and sour pork right for once

Or they may have a new kind of mayonnaise
or cheese which isn't Kraft
Here again   I may depart from my list
kick my heels together
We shall have lunch in the park
We shall have salad and sandwiches
We shall watch baby pull the grass
and rub his teething gums
We shall love every bit of us

None of this is on the list
I probably won't have enough money
for everything   Some of the red peppers
will have to be put back

I don't tell the cashier
why I am smiling
She thinks it might be a beautiful day
She thinks I like the way
she had her hair done
She smiles at the next customer
He thinks this is story policy

When I come home I may find
I've not paid due attention to the list
In buying groceries   as in life
the rewards of transcendence
may be sweet and sour
pork   without the pork

Our Love

We are helpless   now
before this fruiting of your flesh
the pound by pound accretion
of our love on your belly

It is so obvious
like being caught
with one's proverbial pants down
bearing our bedroom tales
into the public eye

Our love rides
on your belly like a watermelon
in the heat of summerlove
So unmistakeable
So delicious

I offer you the parentheses
of my arms
(a small measure of privacy)
and the quietness of knowing
that when the word of our love
has been labouriously spoken
when the porpoise walks
and the penguin has flown
our bodies shall be rooted   still
in each other
and our story
and my pants
still undone

The Peace Poem

The basis for negotiation is slaughter
Animists have slaughtered atheists have
slaughtered Christians have
slaughtered Muslims have
slaughtered B'hai's Catholics have
slaughtered Lutherans Calvinists have
slaughtered Mennonites Communists have
slaughtered Capitalists have Jews Arabs have
slaughtered in person by proxy you have
slaughtered   Yes deep in your heart
if it was not Stalin not Hitler at the very least
you could have throttled the neighbour
whose dog crapped on your lawn
Pacify eliminate put to sleep do away with keep the peace
police capitally punish normalize protect save carry out justice—
these are the words we use to justify
to eulogize our slaughter
These are the strategies of hate
the lies from which
we make ourselves
The only true basis for negotiation
is not righteousness is not strength
is nothing but the slaughter we so euphemize
On our knees let us join
our bloody minds

Sandwich Day

Six a.m. is dry and cold   a slice of brown bread
from the refrigerator   I make lunch   All this is old stuff
    The day goes like cheese   good for me
    boring after weeks of the same consistency
Six p.m. is the last crust   I go home and loaf
around the house   shaking the crumbs out of my head

Earthly Delights & National Visions

*The lemming "overflows from its natural habitat . . . driving
straight forward, the foremost pushed on by those in the rear, the
whole number seemingly obsessed by the desire to forge
ahead."*—Larouse Encyclopedia of Animal Life

he stood quietly
watching the hairy mob around him
stampede bullishly to the edge of the pit-mine
and fling themselves over

they were his enemies the devils
he remembered snide remarks
the final comebacks never ventured
arguments won only in his head

they jostled and pushed their way past him
already there was a twitching heap
dumped on the rocks like a load of warm garbage
blood seeping into the oily water
like a bloom of red algae

they were his friends the fools
he remembered tender moments
understandings never articulated
never understood

he bent his head over like a drunk
looking for a dropped key
there was wheat chaff on his boots
black mud clinging

Eric Reimer, from

In 1913, when Eric Reimer
was a child in the Ukraine,
his family was from East Prussia.
In 1920, as a young boy in Winnipeg,
he was from the Ukraine,
though the family name,
his father explained,
could be traced back to Germany.
About 1939, it was discovered
that the family lineage
actually went back to Holland,
and that the German period was short,
if not nonexistent.
In the early 1940s, intensive perusal
of family documents
suggested the possibility of some Russian blood,
but by 1946 this was clearly demonstrated
to be mere wild conjecture.
During a brief period
while crossing the border
on the way to go shopping in Minneapolis
Eric Reimer was born east of Ottawa.
He later admitted this to be inaccurate,
however; his mother delivered him
somewhere in West Germany
while escaping from the Russians.
In 1965, Eric retired to Abbotsford, B.C.,
where he was from Winnipeg, Manitoba.
He died just two years later
in the Clearbrook shopping center,
where he was from Abbotsford.
After a moment of being
neither here nor there
Eric Reimer appeared in heaven.
There he met God, from Everlasting,
who looked up from the book He was reading
and said, Well then, Eric Reimer,
where are you going?

Brauda Friesen and the Rich Mennonites

Brauda Friesen rose to preach
opened up his Bible wide
opened up his lips like barndoors
let the mares of heaven ride!

How the people sat in wonder
as he preached Woe to the rich!
How they thought that all those *English*
really should be hearing this.

His voice was like an eagle.
Their hearts were on their sleeves.
They knew they'd had a good one
when they all got up to leave.

People thanked him at the doorway
What a work the Lord had done!
People talked of *Brauda* Friesen
all the way from church to home.

Brauda Friesen loved his people.
Brauda Friesen often cried.
No one's sure where Friesen is now,
in an old folks' home, or died.

Only one thing is for certain:
though they praised him for his tongue,
things run just a little smoother
now that *Brauda* Friesen's gone.

The Gift

for Mother, who has survived revolution, civil war, drought,
famine, being orphaned, emigration, servant work,
motherhood, widowhood, and much more besides, on her
75th birthday

After the first sharp cry
it is not a question   this life
of what has been survived
It is what has survived

It is not your father gone
swarthy faces at the window   with guns
In the kitchen   it is Mother's hum
a cup of fresh warm milk   and a bun

It is not Mother reduced to the bone's
terrible whisper   nor a house abandoned
It is the train like a bright snake amid the ruins
a bird soaring   crying   in its flight home

It is not the hopelessness of loss
rude officials at greasy shipyards   and dust
It is a young woman from overseas   the kindness in her face
setting out the doctor's tea in blue china cups

Of that new land as flat as *plautdietsch*
where even *zwieback* loomed significant
and *pluma moos* for all the *englisch* knew
was some kind of deer to shoot

and a horse a husband five bushy-haired
kids a house   several houses   one finally with no steep stairs
a real freezer for meat buns and cookies and a   recreation room
to hide the television   we can really only claim

the cookies   which we did   still frozen
as our first tangible recollection
But even this   our remembering and remembering of remembrance
will pass   and our children's

It is not the quartz-sharp grit deeply clasped
by the heart which we inherit   nor the pain's lingering grasp
It is you   here   now   the rich opaquely buffed layers
of your life   like a pearl   before us

Rolling a Pie Crust

A month after we had sifted our dreams
and spooned our vows
into an overflowing cup
I was in the kitchen
mixing my first pie crust
It was a sticky business
too much water remedied
by too much flour
Tactfully   with a bit of pressure
in the right places
I managed to roll things
if not smooth   at least thin
It was the consummation
that did me in   The dough
stretching comfortably out on the counter
balked at being laid
in a pie pan
It shredded in my palms
like a wet kleenex
I stomped out of the room
out the front door
slamming myself
into the black-bodied night

You watched   perplexed
from the window

I sat crosslegged on the damp   prickly grass
in the company of soft-footed fieldmice
owls
Orion with his sword forever sheathed

When I came to
I was in the kitchen again
thumbing the pieces together on the pie plate

"It's very good" you said   later
watching me cut myself
a modest second piece
"I think so too" I said
spooning extra blueberries over the crust

The Next Ten Years
for Kathy, a tenth anniversary poem

Let us be messy lovers
drunk before breakfast
spilling the white milk everywhere
Let our love be a stain
on the world's tablecloth

Our love is beans
O love we have spilled them
They have grown feet
They are running to the children
running to the neighbours
running to El Salvador
Somalia and Poland
They are nosing underground

They shall come up wantonly
tipsily green   leaning
arms entangled in the wind
clutching a spray of white flowers

Homestead

I built this place,
searched out the strong
green words,
chopped and trimmed them,
chinked them with commas,
thatched a title
between the frozen page
and hardwood frame.

I have been waiting for you
here, beside the fire,
between the lines,
cords of unused words
stacked up around me.
I've left enough unsaid
to keep us warm
all winter.

The Golden Sea
(for Renie and Alan)

The golden sea between the shining seas
oversees the warm bread and steaming porridge
of half the landborne world

is more terrible in its expansive silences
its white-capped storms
than the hair-mad Viking conquests

more demanding of its novices
than the God of Leviticus

above it, the sky is a gigantic blue
examination book
insistently awaiting brilliant expositions

the only reliefs from the relentlessly receding horizon
are windowless lighthouses
and sinking islands
littered with the weatherbeaten hulls and skulls
of foundered pioneers

shipwrecked in Saskatoon
we whisper plots of victory
and escape

we have planted trees

we shall build an ark

Editor's Afterword

Why publish a collection of this sort?

Poetry as an artistic endeavor has been scarce among Mennonite peoples through the centuries. This may be because of their conscious separation from the larger world, or their struggle as an immigrant people, or a general suspicion of the arts held by many members of the groups.

On one hand, "Mennonite" can refer to a subculture with strong traditions of faith and life. On the other hand, "Mennonite" can denote a set of beliefs, held more or less in common by various Christian denominations which include "Mennonite" in their names.

The three poets in this collection are among the finest in the Mennonite peoplehood worldwide, today. The tension between their lives, their particular cultures, and their yearnings has resulted in poetry rich in imagery and full of conviction.

What common themes might a woman from California, a man from eastern Canada, and another from Japan express? Perhaps most basic is an honesty, a bare-bones truthfulness, a disdain for pretense that threads through all the poems. There is also in each a sense of design in which the individual is part of a community—a family, or a tribe, or a people. The cultivation of that embrace is life; the loss of it is crippling, and sometimes even death.

One hears, as well, a wish for peace—with one's spouse, one's past, with all the "beasts" that beset us, both within and without. These poems reach for justice—for both children and Grandpas who are victims, for the misunderstood who can't defend their behavior, for those alive only in our memories who can no longer explain their actions.

While these three poets share an outrage against violence and a devotion to life, the particularity of their voices is clear.

The streams that have shaped Jean Janzen are present in her images—her immigrant heritage and rural childhood, her romance with a man and children, the growing away that so often comes between people. Hers is a view of life seen by a knife-sharp maternal eye. She longs for more time and more warmth. It is her experience with love that brings her both a sense of loss, yet hope.

Yorifumi Yaguchi knows both the lyricism that marks much Japanese verse, as well as the savagery that changed all Japanese who lived through World War II. His harsh images reflect the ravages he has felt; the tension in his lines allows no extravagance and almost no forgiveness. In fact he sees terror and hurt in all of life—between lovers and casual passersby, on the lake and in the woods, within his small child and within himself.

David Waltner-Toews' raw energy exposes the fire of new-married love and the frigid cold of losing one's father. His rollicking lines belie his dismay about those fellow-Mennonites who either never caught the warmth of their community's embrace or too readily cashed it in for respectability. But his is a voice for enduring, for not taking oneself too seriously, for finding the humor in humans' foibles.

Why publish a collection of this sort? We hope that because these three poets have written so well, putting their fingers upon the sadness and the promise that surround them, we might all see the sweep of our own lives more clearly.

—Phyllis Pellman Good

Index